This Journal Belongs to

_____

Date   _____

Aim High Journal

by

Anna Marie McCutchen

Aim High Journal
Copyright © 2015 by Anna Marie McCutchen

Unless otherwise noted, all Scripture quotations are from The
Holy Bible, King James Version (KJV)

Edited by: Anthony Ambrogio
Interior layout: Anthony Ambrogio
Interior images: Microsoft Clipart
Cover design: Walt Nelson
Published by G Publishing, LLC

Library of Congress Control Number: 2015944845

ISBN: 978-0-9862379-6-6

Printed in the United States of America

Introduction

I created this journal as a fun way to plan the rest of your life. The *Aim High Journal* is inspired by the Aim High inspirational song written by Walt Nelson and performed by this writer.

We serve a God who is a planner. He's an organized God. We are created in his image; we are called to use the creative power that's been placed inside of us.

> And God said, "Let us make man in our image, after our likeness: and let them have dominion over the fish of the sea, and over the fowl of the air, and over the cattle, and over all the earth, and over every creeping thing that creepeth upon the earth."
> – Genesis 1:2

Aiming High means doing the best you can with what you have—stirring up the gift that's within you. If you have a mind to Aim High, write down all your ideas and create a strategy for achieving your goals.

How do you inspire yourself to Aim High? One way is to create a vision board on which you visualize how you want yourself to be. Surround yourself with people who are blessed and prosperous. You can even study or read books about successful people who are leading the ideal life you desire to have.

Note: All Biblical quotes in this journal are from the King James Version.

Aim High Journal

Exodus 4:2: And the LORD said unto him, "What is that in thine hand?" And he said, "A rod."

We are fearfully and wonderfully made. God wants us to believe in Him and know that He is able to do miracles through us.

_____

_____

_____

_____

_____

_____

_____

_____

_____

_____

_____

_____

_____

_____

Pursuing your goal is like climbing a ladder—

K1ku-Stock.deviantart.com

Mark 2:4: Since they could not get him to Jesus, because of the crowd, they made an opening.

If your ladder should break, build it back and climb twice higher if achieving your dreams is your desire

_____

_____

_____

_____

_____

_____

Psalm 37:4: Delight thyself also in the Lord; and he shall give thee the desires of thine heart.

Just do it! I used to love that commercial. It's only three simple words: *just—do—it*. We spend ridiculous amounts of time thinking about things we never accomplish. I command a blessing on your life today. If you let God be your architect, what you put your hands to do shall prosper because you have what it takes.

_____

_____

_____

_____

_____

Psalm 1:3: And he shall be like a tree planted by the rivers of the water, that bringeth forth his fruit in his season; his leaf also shall not wither; and whatsoever he doeth shall prosper.

_____

_____

_____

_____

_____

_____

_____

_____

_____

_____

_____

_____

_____

_____

_____

If God is in your heart, all you have to do is ask Him to help you persevere. Anything that's worth having is worth working hard for. Nothing comes easy. You've heard the saying, "Easy come, easy go." Who wants something easy? Really? If you got it easy, you probably wouldn't appreciate it.

If you aim high, you're aiming hard at the same time. The Bible talks about work. If a man doesn't work, he shouldn't eat. Work wasn't intended to be easy. It was intended to be hard. Scripture clearly states "You will work by the sweat of your brow."

_____

_____

_____

_____

_____

_____

_____

_____

_____

The grass may look greener on the other side, but it's really not. Grass is greener when you water it.

You will learn from your mistakes. Don't dwell on the past. Move forward and make better decisions. God wants you to go higher, but you have to change the way you think.

Matthew 9:17: Neither do men put new wine into old bottles: else the bottles break, and the wine runneth out, and the bottles perish: but they put new wine into new bottles, and both are preserved.

New wine, Old bottle

New wine, New bottle

_____

_____

_____

_____

Aim high. Don't look back. Keep moving on when the odds are stacked. If your dreams are big enough, you don't count the facts. Look to the sky and aim high!

_____

_____

_____

_____

_____

_____

_____

_____

_____

_____

You may be wasting too much time trying to reason and make sense out of everything. What's the sense of God giving you a big dream for you to turn around and shut it right down with your doubt? If the Lord gave you the vision, He will also be responsible enough to give you the provision for the vision He places in front of you. Just as God asked Moses, "What is that you have in your hand?", I'm asking you, "What is it that you have in your hand?" You have the ability in your hands to work your vision.

Amos 3:7: Surely the Lord God will do nothing, but he revealeth his secret unto his servants, the prophets.

_____

_____

_____

_____

_____

_____

_____

_____

_____

Many people will try to tear you down on your road to success. Notice that I said *try*. But no weapon ever formed against you shall be able to prosper.

Isiah 54:17: No weapon that is formed against thee shall prosper; and every tongue that shall rise against thee in judgment thou shalt condemn. This is the heritage of the servants of the LORD, and their righteousness is of me, saith the Lord.

Adversity serves as a reminder of how blessed you really are. The devil wouldn't be bothering you if you weren't effective.

_____

_____

_____

_____

_____

_____

_____

_____

_____

_____

_____

The devil peeked into your future and saw how far you are going. He already knows that there's greatness in your life. Ask God to help you be 100 steps or more ahead of the enemy.

Pay your enemies no mind. They are a distraction. You'll pass the test when you master distractions by staying focused. Nehemiah mastered staying focused in spite of his distractions. He refused to let them be the weapon of mass destruction they desired to be. Nehemiah remained successful because he used the tools of praying, working and staying focused.

Nehemiah 6:3: ...I am doing a great work, so that I cannot come down: why should the work cease, whilst I leave it, and come down to you?

_____

_____

_____

_____

_____

_____

_____

_____

_____

_____

_____

_____

_____

_____

_____

_____

_____

_____

_____

_____

_____

Keep moving on when the odds are against you. The adversity you'll face is only because you are getting closer. You have to keep moving. You're driven because you are a precious individual inside of whom God has placed a lot. There are too many gifts in you for you to be stagnant.

1 Corinthians 16:9: For a great door and effectual is opened unto me, and there are many adversaries.

_____

_____

_____

_____

_____

_____

_____

_____

_____

_____

_____

Consider what your greatest obstacles are when climbing the ladder to success, in your attempt to aim high. Do you have people in your circle who are hindering you? Place yourself around blessed, prosperous people who want to see you come up. You need people in your life who are willing to help cultivate what's in you. Who can stimulate your drive? Who can celebrate you, and not just tolerate you?

_____

_____

_____

_____

Find contentment when you are in synch with people, places, and things that you were predestined to connect with, and you'll find divine purpose.

_____

_____

_____

_____

_____

_____

_____

_____

_____

_____

_____

_____

_____

_____

I have a dear friend who spoke something very profound to me. She said, "If you take away your past hurts and your pain, then you're taking away your strength." Don't be ashamed of your testimony. Your past and your pain didn't kill you but made you strong. You've been equipped to be an overcomer. Your faith will take you higher, and with your testimony you will overcome this world.

1 John 5:4: For whatsoever is born of God overcometh the world; and this is the victory that overcometh the world, even our faith.

_____

_____

_____

_____

_____

_____

_____

_____

_____

_____

_____

Dr. Myles Munroe once said, "We must expose God's glory today." Let God dig down through your junk to let his glory out. God is able to get glory even from our dirtiness.

Matthew 5:16: Let your light so shine before men that they may see your good works, and glorify your father which is in heaven.

_____

_____

_____

_____

_____

_____

_____

_____

_____

_____

_____

_____

_____

What God has promised is a sure thing. It is imminent because it's the word of God. He keeps his promises.

_____

_____

_____

_____

_____

_____

_____

_____

_____

_____

_____

_____

_____

_____

Now, being vigilant is still necessary to aim high. The higher you aim, the more the devil will fight.

Matthew 26:41: Watch and pray, that ye enter not into temptation: The spirit indeed is willing, but the flesh is weak.

_____

_____

_____

_____

_____

_____

God is not only springing us forward, He is fast forwarding and exhilarating us. The blessing of the Lord is ready to run you down.

Deuteronomy 28:2: And all these blessings shall come on thee, and overtake thee, if thou shalt hearken onto the voice of the Lord thy God.

_____

_____

_____

_____

_____

Isiah 43:19: Behold, I will do a new thing; now it shall spring forth; shall ye not know it? I will even make a way in the wilderness, and rivers in the desert.

Again, God is hitting the fast-forward button. Give God the praise because even your praise will multiply. Don't pay any attention to the enemies' tactics. If God says yes, no one can say no.

_____

_____

_____

_____

_____

_____

_____

_____

_____

_____

_____

_____

_____

God wants to cause promotion to hit your life. Trust Him to take you to a dimension you have been waiting for. Promotion comes from the Lord.

Psalm 75:6: For promotion cometh neither from the east, nor the west, nor from the south.

_____

_____

_____

_____

_____

_____

_____

_____

_____

_____

_____

_____

_____

_____

Let's go higher in our thinking and our expectations. Let's ask God to take us from surviving to total success.

Ephesians 3:20 Now unto him that is able to do exceeding abundantly above all that we ask or think, according to the power that worketh in us...

_____

_____

_____

_____

_____

_____

_____

_____

_____

_____

_____

_____

_____

_____

Success doesn't happen overnight. You have to survive for the time being until the greater good comes. Do what you have to do until you're able to move forward to bigger and better. Gratitude and contentment show God that you're thankful for where you are, and that will cause God to bless you more.

Philippians 4:12 I know both how to be abased and I know how to abound. Everywhere and in all things I am instructed both to be full and to be hungry, both to abound and to suffer need.

David was anointed by Samuel in the midst of his brothers to be king over Israel. Though he knew who he was he remained humble until his change came, he stayed on the back side of the desert, keeping sheep.

1 Samuel 16:13 Then Samuel took the horn of oil, and anointed him in the midst of his brethren; and the spirit of the Lord came upon David from that day forward...

_____

_____

_____

_____

_____

_____

_____

_____

_____

_____

_____

_____

_____

Discontentment comes when the Lord is nudging you to do more, but you ignore Him. He placed a power in you. He gave you the ability. You can't rest content until you complete the assignment.

Assignment
Completed!

Luke 12:48: For unto whomsoever much is given, of him shall be much required; and to whom men have committed much, of him they will ask more.

Adamant faith and persistence is important when climbing the ladder of success.

Proverbs 13:4: The soul of the sluggard desireth, and hath nothing; but the soul of the diligent shall be made fat.

Proverbs 6:6: Go to the ant, thou sluggard; consider her ways, and be wise.

The ant doesn't have an overseer or a ruler, yet ants have wisdom to prepare for the future.

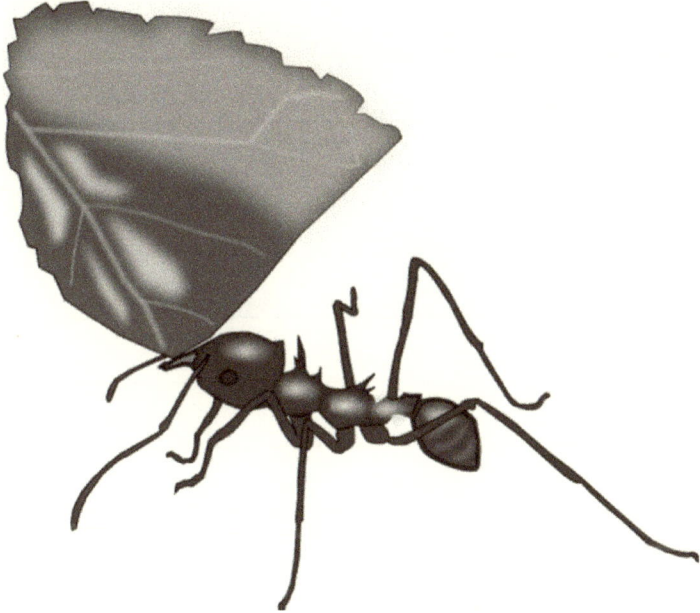

_____

_____

_____

_____

_____

If you want to aim high you definitely must have love in your heart. Ask the Lord to give you a heart of flesh and remove the stony heart.

 Ezekiel 36:26: A new heart also will I give you, and a new spirit will I put within you: and I will take away the stony heart out of your flesh, and I will give you an heart of flesh.

You can't stay in the gutter and rut of negativity and expect the Lord to elevate you. The Lord dwells in high lofty places.

 Isaiah 57:15: For thus saith the high and lofty one that inhabits eternity, whose name is holy, "I dwell in the high and holy place, with him also that is of a contrite and humble spirit, to revive the spirit of the humble, and to revive the heart of the contrite ones."

God wants to set you in high places. At the same time, He doesn't want you high-minded.

_____

_____

_____

_____

_____

_____

_____

_____

_____

_____

_____

_____

_____

_____

When the Lord sets you on high, you will have the ability to comfort the contrite ones. You'll have enough empathy to do so because you have been broken and now blessed.

God can and will take you from height to height as you continue to walk in humility.

_____

_____

_____

_____

_____

_____

_____

_____

_____

_____

_____

_____

_____

_____

Begin to reflect on your brokenness.—how can you soar in ministry and get to where God wants you to be because of the brokenness.

_____

_____

_____

_____

Know your strength.

Know your weakness.

Every time you look back in retrospect, instead of regret, list all the reasons why you will never take back even the hardships of your past and list reasons why you can reflect upon your journal and say, "Yes, Lord"

Caution: Objects in mirror may cause regret.
Don't let them.

Here are some examples of good reasons why you wouldn't take back your harsh experiences and past disappointments:

- Had it not been tough, you wouldn't be a strong survivor today...
- If you take away your past, you take away your strength...

What are *your* reasons?

No matter how old or young you are right now, what do you want to plan for the rest of your life? These are the plans you should write down right now in this journal.

_____

_____

_____

_____

_____

_____

_____

_____

_____

_____

_____

_____

_____

_____

_____

_____

_____

Now that you have refreshed yourself, give yourself a hand and a pat on the back because you have your own self-knowledge, your own ingenuity, and you have bought this journal. Not because you just want to support the author of this journal but because you know you have purpose. Because you must want to aim high in life.

You are battling against the spirit of complacency, and you are investing in the plans for your future. That is something for you to be proud of. That is something to praise God for. God will honor that because He is a planner. The Lord knows the plans He has for you. His hand is on you to organize your life.

What are your highest expectations for the year end?

_____

_____

_____

_____

_____

_____

_____

_____

_____

_____

_____

_____

_____

Use this journal to plan out the rest of your year. (See next 12 pages.)

January

February

March

_____

_____

_____

_____

_____

_____

_____

_____

_____

_____

_____

_____

_____

_____

_____

_____

_____

_____

_____

April

May

June

July

August

_____

_____

_____

_____

_____

_____

_____

_____

_____

_____

_____

_____

_____

_____

_____

_____

_____

September

_____

_____

_____

_____

_____

_____

_____

_____

_____

_____

_____

_____

_____

_____

_____

_____

_____

October

_____

_____

_____

_____

_____

_____

_____

_____

_____

_____

_____

_____

_____

_____

_____

_____

_____

November

December

_____

_____

_____

_____

_____

_____

_____

_____

_____

_____

_____

_____

_____

_____

_____

_____

_____

Plan to aim high

The Lord God is my strength, and he will make my feet like hinds' feet, and he will make me to walk upon mine high places. To the chief singer on my stringed instruments.

Habakkuk 3:19King James Version (KJV)

www.ingramcontent.com/pod-product-compliance
Lightning Source LLC
Chambersburg PA
CBHW030516100426
42813CB00001B/61